FACT CAT

EMILY DAVISON

Izzi Howell

D1394184

FACT CAT

Get your paws on this fantastic new mega-series from Wayland!

Join our Fact Cat on a journey of fun learning about every subject under the sun!

Published in paperback in 2017 by Wayland
Copyright © Hodder and Stoughton 2017

All rights reserved
ISBN: 978 0 7502 9490 4
Dewey Number: 324.6'23'092-dc23
10 9 8 7 6 5 4 3 2 1

MIX
Paper from responsible sources
FSC® C104740

Wayland
An imprint of Hachette Children's Group
Part of Hodder & Stoughton
Carmelite House
50 Victoria Embankment
London EC4Y 0DZ

An Hachette UK Company
www.hachette.co.uk
www.hachettechildrens.co.uk

A catalogue for this title is available from the British Library
Printed and bound in China

Produced for Wayland by
White-Thomson Publishing Ltd
www.wtpub.co.uk

Editor: Izzi Howell
Design: Rocket Design (East Anglia) Ltd
Fact Cat illustrations: Shutterstock/Julien Troneur
Front cover illustration by Wesley Lowe
Consultant: Kate Ruttle

Picture and illustration credits
Alamy: Mary Evans Picture Library 5, Heritage Image Partnership Ltd 7, Trinity Mirror / Mirrorpix 9, Pictorial Press Ltd 11, GL Archive 13, Heritage Image Partnership Ltd 14, Trinity Mirror / Mirrorpix 17t, Lordprice Collection 18; Corbis: Leemage 12, Hulton-Deutsch Collection 19; iStock: Linda Steward 4, EdStock 21; Library of Congress: Bain News Service; Parliamentary Art Collection, WOA S694: 15; Shutterstock: jeff gynane title page, Steve Mann 6, johnbraid 10, Morphart Creation 16, Alhovik 17b, Everett Historical 20.

For more information about the Parliamentary Art Collection see www.parliament.uk/art

Every effort has been made to clear copyright. Should there be any inadvertent omission, please apply to the publisher for rectification.

The author, Izzi Howell, is a writer and editor specialising in children's educational publishing.

The consultant, Kate Ruttle, is a literacy expert and SENCO, and teaches in Suffolk.

FACT CAT FACT

There is a question for you to answer on most spreads in this book. You can check your answers on page 24.

CONTENTS

WHO WAS EMILY DAVISON?

In the early 20th **century**, women in Britain didn't have the same **rights** as men. Some women, such as Emily Davison, thought that this was unfair.

FACT CAT FACT

At the time that Emily Davison was alive, many rich women didn't have jobs. They were expected to stay at home and look after their husbands.

Poor women often worked as maids as well as taking care of their own families.

Emily Davison and a group of women started fighting for women to be allowed to **vote** in **elections**. They wanted to be treated fairly and have their opinions listened to.

Emily Davison was a women's rights **activist**.

EARLY LIFE

Emily Davison was born in England in 1872. At that time, many girls left school before they were 16. However, Emily Davison was able to get a good education.

Emily Davison studied at the Royal Holloway school in London.

Emily Davison went to Oxford University to study Science and English. She got top marks in her final exams. However, she wasn't allowed to **graduate** because she was a woman.

Later, Emily Davison was allowed to graduate from another university. What kind of hat is Emily wearing in this picture?

FACT CAT FACT

Many universities didn't allow **female** students at the beginning of the 20th century. All of their students were men.

7

THE WSPU

In 1906, Emily Davison joined a group called the Women's Social and Political Union (WSPU). The WSPU wanted women in Great Britain to be able to vote.

Emmeline Pankhurst was one of the founders of the WSPU.

The WSPU organised **marches** through towns and cities. They carried **banners** that said 'Votes for Women'.

In 1908, the WSPU organised a huge **protest** in Hyde Park, London. Thousands of people took part.

FACT CAT FACT

Emmeline Pankhurst's daughters were also members of the WSPU. What were their names?

SUFFRAGETTES

Members of the WSPU were called **suffragettes**. The suffragettes often wore purple, white and green clothes.

Today, this woman is dressed up as a suffragette in purple, white and green clothes.

VOTES FOR WOMEN

FACT CAT FACT

The suffragette colours had different meanings. White meant clean and green was a sign of hope. What did purple mean?

The suffragettes made money for their protests by selling newspapers and organising markets. At their markets, they sold clothes and jewellery.

This suffragette is selling newspapers in the centre of London.

BREAKING THE LAW

Many people didn't listen to what the suffragettes were saying. They didn't think that women's rights were important. This made the suffragettes angry and their protests became more **disruptive**.

The suffragettes often broke windows as a protest.

Suffragettes chose to break the **law** so that people would pay attention to them. They often **chained** themselves to railings.

Many women from the WSPU were **arrested** by police for breaking the law.

FACT CAT FACT

In 1910, Emily Davison was arrested for breaking windows in the House of Commons, an important building where the **government** still works today. Which city is the House of Commons in?

PRISON

After being arrested, many of the suffragettes were sent to prison. The suffragettes thought it was worth going to prison if it meant that people listened to what they had to say.

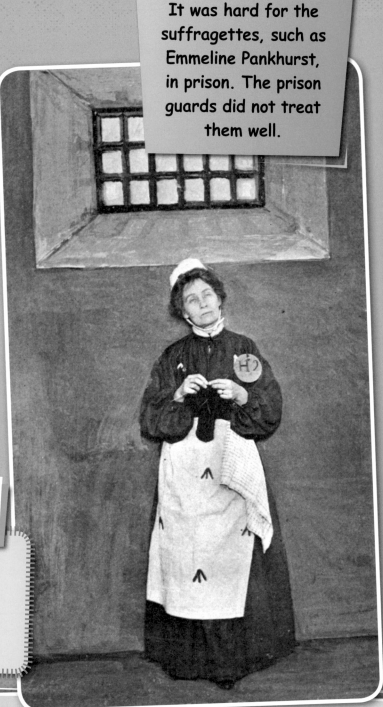

It was hard for the suffragettes, such as Emmeline Pankhurst, in prison. The prison guards did not treat them well.

FACT CAT FACT

Over 1,000 suffragettes went to prison for breaking the law!

Emily Davison went to prison nine times for her protests with the WSPU. Although she had a horrible time in prison, she didn't want to stop protesting until women could vote.

The WSPU gave suffragettes a badge when they left prison. Why are the triangles on the badge purple, white and green?

THE EPSOM DERBY

In June 1913, there was an important horse race near London called the Epsom Derby. King George V of England came to watch his horse take part in the race.

Thousands of people came to watch the Epsom Derby in 1913.

Emily Davison decided that the Epsom Derby would be a good place to protest for women's right to vote. When the king's horse came near her on the **track**, Emily Davison ran in front of it.

One of the first film cameras recorded the moment that Emily Davison ran in front of the king's horse. Can you find out the name of the horse?

PHIL COOPER

FACT CAT FACT

Emily Davison may have been trying to put a suffragette flag on the horse as a protest.

AFTER THE HORSE RACE

Emily Davison was taken to hospital, but she died four days later. Today, most people think that she was trying to take part in a protest and that she died by accident.

The WSPU wrote about Emily Davison's death in 'The Suffragette' newspaper.

"The Suffragette," June 13, 1913.

Registered at the G.P.O. as a Newspaper

The Suffragette

Edited by Christabel Pankhurst.

The Official Organ of the Women's Social and Political Union

No. 35 — Vol. 1.   FRIDAY, JUNE 13, 1913.   Price 1d. Weekly (Post Free) 1½d.

LOVE THAT OVERCOMETH

IN HONOUR AND IN LOVING, REVERENT MEMORY
OF
EMILY WILDING DAVISON.
SHE DIED FOR WOMEN.
"Greater love hath no man than this, that he lay down his life for his friends."
Miss Davison, who made a protest at the Derby against the denial of Votes to Women, was knocked down by the King's horse and sustained terrible injuries of which she died on Sunday, June 8th, 1913.

Thousands of people went to Emily Davison's funeral. They were sad that Emily died and that nothing had changed.

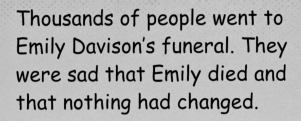
Suffragettes carried banners and marched with Emily Davison's **coffin**.

EDWAR NEWLING

FIGHT ON & GOD WILL GIVE THE VICTORY

FACT CAT FACT

Emily Davison was buried in the north of England. Which important WSPU words are written on her **gravestone**?

WOMEN'S RIGHTS TODAY

When the **First World War** started in 1914, most suffragettes stopped protesting. They were busy working, as women had to do men's jobs as well as their own while the men were away fighting.

When the war finished in 1918, women over the age of 30 were allowed to vote in Britain. Men could vote at 21.

FACT CAT FACT

In 1928, the law was changed and women could vote when they were 21 years old. Finally British women had the same voting rights as men!

Today, women have many more rights. In most countries, they can vote at the age of 18, just like men. Many women work in governments around the world.

In Germany, a woman called Angela Merkel is in charge of the government.

QUIZ

Try to answer the questions below. Look back through the book to help you. Check your answers on page 24.

1 Which subjects did Emily Davison study at university?

a) Art and History
b) English and Science
c) Maths and Geography

2 Emily Davison joined the WSPU in 1906. True or not true?

a) true
b) not true

3 What colours did the suffragettes wear?

a) red, white and blue
b) yellow, blue and purple
c) purple, white and green

4 Suffragettes never broke the law. True or not true?

a) true
b) not true

5 How many times did Emily Davison go to prison?

a) three
b) nine
c) twelve

6 Emily Davison died before women were able to vote. True or not true?

a) true
b) not true

GLOSSARY

activist someone who tries to change society

arrested to be taken by the police and asked questions about a crime

banner a long piece of cloth stretched between two poles with words written on it

century a period of 100 years. The 20th century refers to dates between 1900 and 1999.

chain to join something or someone to a place using a piece of metal

coffin the box that a dead body is buried in

disruptive describes a way of doing something to get attention

election the time when people vote to choose the leader of their country

female describes a woman

First World War a war fought between many European countries from 1914 to 1918

founder the person that starts an organisation

government the group of people that are in charge of a country

graduate to study for and receive a degree from a university

gravestone the stone on top of a grave that shows the name of the person buried there

laws the rules of a country

march an organised walk by a group to show that they don't agree with something

protest to show that you disagree with something

rights the things that you can do or have, according to the laws of your country

suffragette a woman who protested for other women to be able to vote in elections

track the path used for races

vote to choose the person that you want to be in charge of your country

INDEX

ANSWERS

Pages 7–19

page 7: A mortar board hat that people wear when they graduate.

page 9: Christabel, Sylvia and Adela

page 10: Purple stood for dignity.

page 13: London

page 15: Purple, white and green are the suffragette colours.

page 17: Anmer

page 19: 'Deeds not words'

Quiz answers

1   b - English and Science

2   true

3   c - purple, white and green

4   not true – suffragettes sometimes broke the law as a protest.

5   b - nine

6   true